ALL MY LIFE

EVERYTHING "YOU" NEED TO KNOW AFTER "I" GO...

AN END-OF-LIFE GUIDE TO HELP YOU WITH DECISIONS, DISCUSSIONS, AND FINAL PREPARATIONS

S. TRAA

Copyright © S. Traa 2022 - All rights reserved.

The content contained within this book may not be reproduced, duplicated, or transmitted without direct written permission from the author or the publisher. Under no circumstances will any blame or legal responsibility be held against the publisher, or author, for any damages, reparation, or monetary loss due to the information contained within this book. Either directly or indirectly. You are responsible for your own choices, actions, and results.

Legal Notice:

This book is copyright protected. This book is only for personal use. You cannot amend, distribute, sell, use, quote, or paraphrase any part, or the content within this book, without the consent of the author or publisher.

Disclaimer Notice:

Please note the information contained within this document is for educational and entertainment purposes only. All effort has been executed to present accurate, up-to-date, and reliable, complete information. No warranties of any kind are declared or implied. Readers acknowledge that the author is not engaging in the rendering of legal, financial, medical, or professional advice. The content within this book has been derived from various sources. Please consult a licensed professional before attempting any techniques outlined in this book.

By reading this document, the reader agrees that under no circumstances is the author responsible for any losses, direct or indirect, which are incurred as a result of the use of the information contained within this document, including, but not limited to, — errors, omissions, or inaccuracies.

All Quotes belong to their respective owners and I do not own any of them. Each has been taken from the following citation:

Norbert Juma, Lead Editor. (2022, April 18). Funny Inspirational Quotes Celebrating Life, Love & Struggles. Everyday Power. https://everydaypower.com/funny-motivational-quotes-about-life/

! IMMEDIATE ACTION !

In the event of my passing, please deliver this particular book immediately to:

Name:

_____

Address:

_____

_____

Email Address:

_____

Phone:

_____

Note: Kindly note that this planner is NOT a legal document nor a will. It does not replace a will or a testament.

MY FINAL WORDS

I Am Pouring My Heart Out and Leaving Nothing Behind; The Good, The Bad, and the Indifferent...

My Cherished Loved Ones:

1.

_____

_____

_____

2.

_____

_____

_____

3.

_____

_____

_____

★★★★★

*If you like this book, please **leave a review on Amazon** because it will help me improve it in the future and help other people just like you to narrate their final words.*

CONTENTS

1. My First Instructions — 1
2. My Personal Details — 19
3. Vital Data and Document's Location — 24
4. Financials and Business — 35
5. Personal Belongings & Credentials — 53
6. Dependants, Pets, and Contacts — 59
7. Hobbies and Interests — 70
8. Things That Made Me Proud — 82
9. Things I Wish I Did Differently — 96
10. Faith, Belief, and Spirituality — 110
11. The Fulfilled Dreams — 120
12. Being Grateful — 133
13. Life Support and Resuscitation — 147
14. Funeral Arrangements — 151
15. My Life's Story & Obituary — 158
16. The Donor — 166
17. My Final Thoughts — 170
18. Farewell Wishes — 179

Extra Notes — 187

A QUOTE TO LIVE BY

I always wanted to be somebody,

but now I realize I should have been more specific.

LILY TOMLIN

CHAPTER 1
MY FIRST INSTRUCTIONS

I understand the gravity of the situation and the uprising grief you may be facing due to my departure, my beloved; however, there are a few things I want you to do before moving forward. And, you can't say NO as I have already passed on, ha! I request you to take care of the following things. Once you fulfill each instruction, please check off the box next to it for double confirmation.

Thank you

☐ #1. Acquire my death certificate and list the details below:

- Agency Name:
  _____

- Date of Death:
  _____

- Registration Number:
  _____

☐ #2. Inform my friends and family about my departure.

- Name and Contact Information:
  _____

- Name and Contact Information:
  _____

- Name and Contact Information:
  _____

- Name and Contact Information:
  _____

- Name and Contact Information:
  _____

- Name and Contact Information:
  _____

MY FIRST INSTRUCTIONS

- Name and Contact Information:
  _____

- Name and Contact Information:
  _____

- Name and Contact Information:
  _____

- Name and Contact Information:
  _____

- Name and Contact Information:
  _____

- Name and Contact Information:
  _____

- Name and Contact Information:
  _____

- Name and Contact Information:
  _____

- Name and Contact Information:
  _____

☐ #3. Please secure my owned properties and vehicles.

- Property/Vehicle Name and Location:
  _____

- Property/Vehicle Name and Location:
  _____

- Property/Vehicle Name and Location:
  _____

- Property/Vehicle Name and Location:
  _____

- Property/Vehicle Name and Location:
  _____

- Property/Vehicle Name and Location:
  _____

- Property/Vehicle Name and Location:
  _____

- Property/Vehicle Name and Location:
  _____

- Property/Vehicle Name and Location:
  _____

MY FIRST INSTRUCTIONS

☐ #4. Please throw out the food lying around.

☐ #5. Secure my valuables.

- Valuables and Location:
  _____

- Valuables and Location:
  _____

- Valuables and Location:
  _____

- Valuables and Location:
  _____

- Valuables and Location:
  _____

- Valuables and Location:
  _____

- Valuables and Location:
  _____

- Valuables and Location:
  _____

- Valuables and Location:
  _____

☐ #6. Forward farewell mail to my friends and family members on my behalf.

- The contents of my farewell mail:

_____
_____
_____
_____
_____
_____
_____
_____
_____
_____
_____
_____
_____
_____
_____
_____
_____

MY FIRST INSTRUCTIONS

ALL MY LIFE

_____
_____
_____
_____
_____
_____
_____
_____
_____
_____
_____
_____
_____

Thank you for everything! I will remember you always...

_____

MY FIRST INSTRUCTIONS

☐ #7. Notify my employer about my departure and ask if there is any:

- Outstanding pay

_____

_____

_____

- Life Insurance Policy

_____

_____

_____

☐ #8. Obtain the will and contact the executer or the lawyer

- Location of the will:

_____

_____

_____

Contact Information of the lawyer/executer:

Name: _____

Contact: _____

☐ #9. Apply for the Grant of Probate.

☐ #10. Open an Estate Bank Account and notify my lawyer to take assigned actions:

- ☐ Settle my remaining debts
- ☐ Pay off my taxes
- ☐ Distribute all my assets according to the will

☐ #11. Please make an inventory of all my owned assets, starting with this journal.

☐ _____

☐ _____

☐ _____

☐ _____

☐ _____

☐ _____

☐ _____

☐ _____

☐ _____

☐ _____

☐ _____

☐ _____

☐ _____

☐ _____

MY FIRST INSTRUCTIONS

- [ ] _____
- [ ] _____
- [ ] _____
- [ ] _____
- [ ] _____
- [ ] _____
- [ ] _____
- [ ] _____
- [ ] _____
- [ ] _____
- [ ] _____
- [ ] _____
- [ ] _____
- [ ] _____
- [ ] _____
- [ ] _____
- [ ] _____
- [ ] _____
- [ ] _____
- [ ] _____
- [ ] _____

ALL MY LIFE

☐ _____

☐ _____

☐ _____

☐ _____

☐ _____

☐ _____

☐ _____

☐ _____

☐ _____

☐ _____

☐ _____

☐ _____

☐ _____

☐ _____

☐ _____

☐ #12. Pay off my bills and cancel my services.

- Bill/Service and Credentials:

  _____

- Bill/Service and Credentials:

  _____

MY FIRST INSTRUCTIONS

- Bill/Service and Credentials:
  _____

- Bill/Service and Credentials:
  _____

- Bill/Service and Credentials:
  _____

- Bill/Service and Credentials:
  _____

- Bill/Service and Credentials:
  _____

- Bill/Service and Credentials:
  _____

- Bill/Service and Credentials:
  _____

☐ #13. I want the following people to be my pall-bearers, please let them know:

- Name and Contact Information:
  _____

- Name and Contact Information:
  _____

- Name and Contact Information:
  _____

- Name and Contact Information:
  _____

- Name and Contact Information:
  _____

- Name and Contact Information:
  _____

- Name and Contact Information:
  _____

- Name and Contact Information:
  _____

MY FIRST INSTRUCTIONS

☐ #14. Please cancel the following things.

- Things to be cancelled and Credentials:
  _____

- Things to be cancelled and Credentials:
  _____

- Things to be cancelled and Credentials:
  _____

- Things to be cancelled and Credentials:
  _____

- Things to be cancelled and Credentials:
  _____

- Things to be cancelled and Credentials:
  _____

- Things to be cancelled and Credentials:
  _____

- Things to be cancelled and Credentials:
  _____

- Things to be cancelled and Credentials:
  _____

☐ #15. List of people who owed me money, please collect it.

ALL MY LIFE

- Name, Amount Owed, and Contact Information:

_____

_____

- Name, Amount Owed, and Contact Information:

_____

_____

- Name, Amount Owed, and Contact Information:

_____

_____

- Name, Amount Owed, and Contact Information:

_____

_____

- Name, Amount Owed, and Contact Information:

_____

_____

Note for the writer:

The information listed above is to help your beloved people to get through difficult times with ease. There may be a few changes in the entire process based on the region. Please research and try to learn the requirements and make changes in this journal accordingly.

— Thank You!

A QUOTE TO LIVE BY

Don't worry about the world coming to an end today.

It is already tomorrow in Australia.

CHARLES SCHULZ

CHAPTER 2
MY PERSONAL DETAILS

This is the section where I will be revealing my personal identity along with other important details. Don't get surprised if you find something you didn't know about, it was personal unless I was summoned by the God.

#1. Full Legal Name:

_____

#2. Gender:

_____

#3: Maiden Name:

_____

#4: Date of Birth:

_____

. . .

#5: Race:

_____

#6: Place of Birth:

_____

#7: Birth Certificate Number:

_____

#8: Social Insurance Number/Social Security Number:

_____

#9: Phone No:

_____

#10: Email Addresses and Passwords:

_____

_____

_____

_____

_____

_____

MY PERSONAL DETAILS

#11: Primary Residence:

_____

#12: Other Owned Residences:

I)

_____

II)

_____

III)

_____

IV)

_____

#13: Father's Name:

_____

#14: Father's Birth Place:

_____

#15: Mother's Name:

_____

#16: Mother's Birth Place:

_____

#17: Medical Card details:

_____

_____

_____

#18: Marital Status:

_____

#19: Name of the Spouse:

_____

#20: My Passport Number:

_____

#21: Country of Passport:

_____

#22: Healthcare Number:

_____

#23: Additional Information:

_____

_____

_____

_____

A QUOTE TO LIVE BY

Opportunity does not knock;

it presents itself when you beat down the door.

KYLE CHANDLER

CHAPTER 3
VITAL DATA AND DOCUMENT'S LOCATION

I will be making a list of all my important documents that you need to acquire from the specified locations. There will be additional important information regarding those documents so watch out, handle my documents carefully okay.

#1: Important Documents

- Group and Club Memberships

_____

_____

_____

_____

VITAL DATA AND DOCUMENT'S LOCATION

- Honors and Awards

_____

_____

_____

_____

_____

- Marriage

_____

_____

_____

- Birth

_____

_____

- Divorce

_____

_____

_____

ALL MY LIFE

- Wills

- Trusts

- Lawyers

- Vehicle Registrations, Titles, and Other

_____
_____
_____
_____
_____

- Adoption and Other Certificates

_____
_____
_____
_____

- Miscellaneous

_____
_____
_____
_____
_____
_____

#2: Additional information and special instructions regarding the documents, and a few other things:

VITAL DATA AND DOCUMENT'S LOCATION

#3: I would like to elaborate on educational and employment history:

- My Educational History:

VITAL DATA AND DOCUMENT'S LOCATION

My Employment History:

VITAL DATA AND DOCUMENT'S LOCATION

A QUOTE TO LIVE BY

Better to remain silent and be thought a fool

than to speak out and remove all doubt.

ABRAHAM LINCOLN

CHAPTER 4
FINANCIALS AND BUSINESS

It is important to me that I illustrate my life-long financials and business interests. Here, I will be mentioning my both personal and business financials, investments, and more. Do not compare my financials with yours, you will get there...

☐ #1: My personal bank accounts:

Bank Name and Account Number

_____

Bank Name and Account Number

_____

Bank Name and Account Number

_____

☐ #2: My business bank accounts:

Bank Name and Account Number

_____

Bank Name and Account Number

_____

Bank Name and Account Number

_____

- Additional information regarding bank accounts:

_____
_____
_____
_____
_____
_____
_____
_____
_____
_____
_____

FINANCIALS AND BUSINESS

☐ #3: Mortgages

Taken on, Total Amount, Paid, Pending, and Mortgage Provider

_____

_____

_____

Taken on, Total Amount, Paid, Pending, and Mortgage Provider

_____

_____

_____

Taken on, Total Amount, Paid, Pending, and Mortgage Provider

_____

_____

_____

Taken on, Total Amount, Paid, Pending, and Mortgage Provider

_____

_____

_____

Taken on, Total Amount, Paid, Pending, and Mortgage Provider

_____

_____

_____

- Additional Information About my mortgages

FINANCIALS AND BUSINESS

☐ #4: Safety Deposit Box

Bank, Deposit Key, Location, Items

_____

_____

_____

Bank, Deposit Key, Location, Items

_____

_____

_____

Bank, Deposit Key, Location, Items

_____

_____

_____

Bank, Deposit Key, Location, Items

_____

_____

_____

☐ **#5: Storage Lockers**

Locker Identification, Keys, Location, Items

_____

_____

_____

Locker Identification, Keys, Location, Items

_____

_____

_____

Locker Identification, Keys, Location, Items

_____

_____

_____

Locker Identification, Keys, Location, Items

_____

_____

_____

FINANCIALS AND BUSINESS

☐ #6: My Business Interests

ALL MY LIFE

FINANCIALS AND BUSINESS

☐ #7: Mentioning all the Debts and Loans to My Name

Debt or Loan, Total Amount, Paid, Pending, Provider

_____

_____

_____

Debt or Loan, Total Amount, Paid, Pending, Provider

_____

_____

_____

Debt or Loan, Total Amount, Paid, Pending, Provider

_____

_____

_____

Debt or Loan, Total Amount, Paid, Pending, Provider

_____

_____

_____

ALL MY LIFE

☐ #8: List of All My Insurance Policies

Provider, Plan, Amount Benefits and Claim

_____

_____

Provider, Plan, Amount Benefits and Claim

_____

_____

Provider, Plan, Amount Benefits and Claim

_____

_____

Provider, Plan, Amount Benefits and Claim

_____

_____

Provider, Plan, Amount Benefits and Claim

_____

_____

Provider, Plan, Amount Benefits and Claim

_____

_____

FINANCIALS AND BUSINESS

☐ #9: List of all owned credit cards

Provider, Location of Card, Type and Credentials, Instructions

_____

_____

Provider, Location of Card, Type and Credentials, Instructions

_____

_____

Provider, Location of Card, Type and Credentials, Instructions

_____

_____

Provider, Location of Card, Type and Credentials, Instructions

_____

_____

Provider, Location of Card, Type and Credentials, Instructions

_____

_____

Provider, Location of Card, Type and Credentials, Instructions

_____

_____

ALL MY LIFE

☐ #10: Pension related instructions (what to do with it?)

FINANCIALS AND BUSINESS

☐ #11: Information about my income and property taxes

ALL MY LIFE

☐ #12: List of all my bills and utilities

☐ _____
☐ _____
☐ _____
☐ _____
☐ _____
☐ _____
☐ _____
☐ _____
☐ _____
☐ _____
☐ _____
☐ _____
☐ _____
☐ _____
☐ _____
☐ _____
☐ _____
☐ _____
☐ _____
☐ _____
☐ _____
☐ _____
☐ _____
☐ _____
☐ _____
☐ _____

FINANCIALS AND BUSINESS

☐ #13: Please acquire my following investments

Investment Type, Credentials, Successor, and Instructions

_____

_____

_____

_____

Investment Type, Credentials, Successor, and Instructions

_____

_____

_____

_____

Investment Type, Credentials, Successor, and Instructions

_____

_____

_____

_____

Investment Type, Credentials, Successor, and Instructions

_____

_____

_____

_____

Investment Type, Credentials, Successor, and Instructions

_____

_____

_____

Investment Type, Credentials, Successor, and Instructions

_____

_____

_____

Investment Type, Credentials, Successor, and Instructions

_____

_____

_____

Investment Type, Credentials, Successor, and Instructions

_____

_____

_____

Investment Type, Credentials, Successor, and Instructions

_____

_____

_____

FINANCIALS AND BUSINESS

A QUOTE TO LIVE BY

If you're going to tell people the truth,

be funny or they'll kill you.

BILLY WILDER

CHAPTER 5
PERSONAL BELONGINGS & CREDENTIALS

☐ #1: Please obtain my personal belongings from the said location and make the best use of them.

Wallets

_____

_____

Purses

_____

_____

Keys

_____

_____

Jewellery

_____

_____

Cash

_____

_____

Watches

_____

_____

Books

_____

_____

Phone and other electronic devices

_____

_____

_____

Records

_____

_____

PERSONAL BELONGINGS & CREDENTIALS

Wardrobe

_____

_____

Paintings and other art related items

_____

_____

Other

_____

_____

_____

_____

_____

_____

_____

_____

_____

☐ #2: Use the following login credentials to access various owned softwares and accounts:

Software/Account, Login credentials or passwords, and Instructions

_____

_____

Software/Account, Login credentials or passwords, and Instructions

_____

_____

Software/Account, Login credentials or passwords, and Instructions

_____

_____

Software/Account, Login credentials or passwords, and Instructions

_____

_____

Software/Account, Login credentials or passwords, and Instructions

_____

_____

Software/Account, Login credentials or passwords, and Instructions

_____

_____

· · ·

PERSONAL BELONGINGS & CREDENTIALS

Software/Account, Login credentials or passwords, and Instructions

_____

_____

Software/Account, Login credentials or passwords, and Instructions

_____

_____

Software/Account, Login credentials or passwords, and Instructions

_____

_____

Software/Account, Login credentials or passwords, and Instructions

_____

_____

Software/Account, Login credentials or passwords, and Instructions

_____

_____

Software/Account, Login credentials or passwords, and Instructions

_____

_____

Software/Account, Login credentials or passwords, and Instructions

_____

A QUOTE TO LIVE BY

When I hear somebody sigh, Life is hard,

I am always tempted to ask, 'Compared to what?'.

SYDNEY HARRIS

CHAPTER 6
DEPENDANTS, PETS, AND CONTACTS

Throughout my life, I tried helping as many people as I could, thus, I do have a few dependants. I request you to inform them about my departure and please try to take care of them even after I am gone. Furthermore, I also have a few loyal and enthusiastic pets that made me smile during my toughest times. I would hate to see them sad, please keep them happy.

☐ #1: List of dependants that needs to be informed and catered to, after my departure:

Dependant's Name, Contact, and Additional Information

_____

_____

_____

_____

. . .

Dependant's Name, Contact, and Additional Information

_____

_____

_____

_____

Dependant's Name, Contact, and Additional Information

_____

_____

_____

_____

Dependant's Name, Contact, and Additional Information

_____

_____

_____

_____

- Additional information about the dependants and things you need to know

_____

_____

_____

DEPENDANTS, PETS, AND CONTACTS

☐ #2: Information about my pets and instructions on how to take care of them:

Pet Type and Name, Likes and Dislikes, Caring Information

_____

_____

_____

_____

Pet Type and Name, Likes and Dislikes, Caring Information

_____

_____

_____

_____

Pet Type and Name, Likes and Dislikes, Caring Information

_____

_____

_____

_____

Pet Type and Name, Likes and Dislikes, Caring Information

_____

_____

_____

_____

ALL MY LIFE

- A few extra things about my pets

☐ #3: Here is a list of every person who maintained a good relationship with me throughout my life. Please keep in touch with them:

Name and Contact Information

_____

_____

Name and Contact Information

_____

_____

Name and Contact Information

_____

_____

Name and Contact Information

_____

_____

Name and Contact Information

_____

_____

Name and Contact Information

_____

_____

. . .

ALL MY LIFE

Name and Contact Information

_____

_____

Name and Contact Information

_____

_____

Name and Contact Information

_____

_____

Name and Contact Information

_____

_____

Name and Contact Information

_____

_____

Name and Contact Information

_____

_____

Name and Contact Information

_____

_____

DEPENDANTS, PETS, AND CONTACTS

Name and Contact Information

_____

_____

Name and Contact Information

_____

_____

Name and Contact Information

_____

_____

Name and Contact Information

_____

_____

Name and Contact Information

_____

_____

Name and Contact Information

_____

_____

Name and Contact Information

_____

_____

ALL MY LIFE

Name and Contact Information

_____

_____

Name and Contact Information

_____

_____

Name and Contact Information

_____

_____

Name and Contact Information

_____

_____

Name and Contact Information

_____

_____

Name and Contact Information

_____

_____

Name and Contact Information

_____

_____

DEPENDANTS, PETS, AND CONTACTS

Name and Contact Information

_____

_____

Name and Contact Information

_____

_____

Name and Contact Information

_____

_____

Name and Contact Information

_____

_____

Name and Contact Information

_____

_____

Name and Contact Information

_____

_____

Name and Contact Information

_____

_____

ALL MY LIFE

Name and Contact Information

___

___

Name and Contact Information

___

___

Name and Contact Information

___

___

Name and Contact Information

___

___

Name and Contact Information

___

___

Name and Contact Information

___

___

A QUOTE TO LIVE BY

The elevator to success is out of order.

You'll have to use the stairs. one step at a time.

JOE GIRARD

CHAPTER 7
HOBBIES AND INTERESTS

I lived a good life and there are many things that make me proud as I jot down things into this journal. Furthermore, I was also keen on numerous hobbies that stimulated various aspects of my life; I think those will be worth mentioning.

I.

_____

_____

_____

_____

_____

_____

HOBBIES AND INTERESTS

2.

3.

ALL MY LIFE

4.

5.

HOBBIES AND INTERESTS

6.

7.

ALL MY LIFE

8.

9.

HOBBIES AND INTERESTS

10.

11.

ALL MY LIFE

12.

13.

HOBBIES AND INTERESTS

14.

15.

16.

17.

HOBBIES AND INTERESTS

18.

19.

ALL MY LIFE

20.

21.

A QUOTE TO LIVE BY

The best way to cheer yourself up

is to try to cheer someone else up.

MARK TWAIN

CHAPTER 8
THINGS THAT MADE ME PROUD

As I mentioned earlier, there are things that I did in my life that made me extremely proud of myself and my existence. If it wasn't for all these things, I wouldn't have been happier. Looking back, I don't care how small or big these things appear to the world, but they made me smile and most importantly, proud. If you could read and duplicate a few of them in your life, I know you will be happier in your final moments as well.

1.

_____

_____

_____

_____

THINGS THAT MADE ME PROUD

2.

_____

_____

_____

_____

_____

_____

_____

_____

3.

_____

_____

_____

_____

_____

_____

_____

_____

ALL MY LIFE

4.

5.

THINGS THAT MADE ME PROUD

6.

7.

ALL MY LIFE

8.

9.

THINGS THAT MADE ME PROUD

10.

11.

12.

13.

THINGS THAT MADE ME PROUD

14.

15.

ALL MY LIFE

16.

17.

THINGS THAT MADE ME PROUD

18.

19.

ALL MY LIFE

20.

21.

THINGS THAT MADE ME PROUD

22.

23.

ALL MY LIFE

24.

25.

A QUOTE TO LIVE BY

The minute you settle for less than you deserve,

you get even less than you settled for.

MAUREEN DOWD

CHAPTER 9
THINGS I WISH I DID DIFFERENTLY

Despite the things that made me happy, I also indulged myself in a few activities that made me question the decisions I took back then; I am not perfect after all. It is more crucial to me that I state the things that could have been dealt with differently. So that you or anybody else who reads my journal doesn't repeat the same mistake as me; here they are:

I.

_____

_____

_____

_____

_____

THINGS I WISH I DID DIFFERENTLY

2.

3.

ALL MY LIFE

4.

5.

THINGS I WISH I DID DIFFERENTLY

6.

7.

8.

9.

THINGS I WISH I DID DIFFERENTLY

10.

11.

12.

13.

14.

15.

ALL MY LIFE

16.

17.

18.

19.

ALL MY LIFE

20.

21.

THINGS I WISH I DID DIFFERENTLY

22.

23.

24.

25.

A QUOTE TO LIVE BY

The key to success is not through achievement but through enthusiasm.

MALCOLM FORBES

CHAPTER 10
FAITH, BELIEF, AND SPIRITUALITY

I wasn't a saint at all, but I did believe in the power of my decisions and the existence of a higher power that looks after us all. You may name it God or the universe, but most importantly, you should believe in yourself; at least that is what I learned in my own way. My faith, belief system, and spirituality were all one tracked and I would love to share it with you my dear.

☐ #1: Personal faith metrics and the things that I had most faith in my life, and why.

_____

_____

_____

_____

_____

FAITH, BELIEF, AND SPIRITUALITY

ALL MY LIFE

FAITH, BELIEF, AND SPIRITUALITY

☐ #2: My belief system that helped me stay put during various challenging situations.

ALL MY LIFE

FAITH, BELIEF, AND SPIRITUALITY

☐ #3: My spirituality was unique to me in different ways. Here's what I knew or learned about it:

_____
_____
_____
_____
_____
_____
_____
_____
_____
_____
_____
_____
_____
_____
_____
_____
_____
_____
_____
_____
_____
_____

FAITH, BELIEF, AND SPIRITUALITY

ALL MY LIFE

A QUOTE TO LIVE BY

If you think you are too small to be effective,

you have never been in the dark with a mosquito.

BETTY REESE

CHAPTER 11
THE FULFILLED DREAMS

My belief strengthened my ability to dream and prosper. Due to this, I was able to achieve so many of my dreams. No matter what you do from here on out, please do yourself a favor and set some dreams for your life. And one more thing, money is not a dream. You cannot justify having cash with a dream. It certainly makes life easier, but your real dream happens after you get your money; it is what you do with it that counts. I earned my share of money and trust me you will be happier with following your heart and achieving your passion. Let me walk you through some of my fulfilled dreams:

THE FULFILLED DREAMS

1.

2.

ALL MY LIFE

3.

4.

THE FULFILLED DREAMS

5.

6.

ALL MY LIFE

7.

8.

THE FULFILLED DREAMS

9.

10.

ALL MY LIFE

I was able to set many dreams for myself, some turned to reality while few remained. I am not sad though, because hey, that is life; it is unpredictable and I liked it that way. Don't let this rule of life stop you from setting big dreams for yourself. I would encourage you with all my heart to see dreams and do everything in your power to achieve them. Now, I will tell you about the dreams that I did set but was never able to fulfill, however, the process of attainment still made me happy. It's always the process, isn't it? Never the outcome.

I.

_____

_____

_____

_____

_____

_____

_____

_____

_____

THE FULFILLED DREAMS

2.

___

3.

___

ALL MY LIFE

4.

5.

THE FULFILLED DREAMS

6.

7.

ALL MY LIFE

8.

9.

THE FULFILLED DREAMS

10.

A QUOTE TO LIVE BY

The difference between genius and stupidity is;

genius has its limits.

ALBERT EINSTEIN

CHAPTER 12
BEING GRATEFUL

Life may have given me melons like everyone else, but I was also blessed with so many things, events, and people that I am deeply grateful for, to this day. It will be unfair to myself if I don't take the time to mention the things that I was blessed with;

I AM GRATEFUL FOR...

1.

_____

_____

_____

_____

_____

ALL MY LIFE

2.

3.

4.

5.

ALL MY LIFE

6.

7.

8.

9.

ALL MY LIFE

10.

11.

12.

13.

ALL MY LIFE

14.

15.

BEING GRATEFUL

16.

17.

ALL MY LIFE

18.

19.

BEING GRATEFUL

20.

21.

ALL MY LIFE

22.

23.

24.

25.

A QUOTE TO LIVE BY

Always borrow money from a pessimist.

He won't expect it back.

OSCAR WILDE

CHAPTER 13
LIFE SUPPORT AND RESUSCITATION

I feel strongly towards providing myself with life support and other medical facilities. Moreso, I have something to say about my resuscitation as well. Let me tell you what I feel:

_____

_____

_____

_____

_____

_____

_____

_____

_____

ALL MY LIFE

LIFE SUPPORT AND RESUSCITATION

A QUOTE TO LIVE BY

Opportunity is missed by most people because it is dressed in overalls and looks like work.

THOMAS EDISON

CHAPTER 14
FUNERAL ARRANGEMENTS

You can use this section of my journal to complete my funeral arrangements. Please list down all the things required along with the correct procedure for my final departure. It will help me live at peace in the afterlife.

☐ #1: Basic information of the funeral home

Name:

_____

Address:

_____

_____

Contact:

_____

_____

• • •

ALL MY LIFE

☐ #2: List down all the items necessary for my funeral

- ☐ _____
- ☐ _____
- ☐ _____
- ☐ _____
- ☐ _____
- ☐ _____
- ☐ _____
- ☐ _____
- ☐ _____
- ☐ _____
- ☐ _____
- ☐ _____
- ☐ _____
- ☐ _____
- ☐ _____
- ☐ _____
- ☐ _____
- ☐ _____
- ☐ _____
- ☐ _____
- ☐ _____
- ☐ _____
- ☐ _____
- ☐ _____
- ☐ _____
- ☐ _____
- ☐ _____
- ☐ _____
- ☐ _____

FUNERAL ARRANGEMENTS

☐ #3: Please list down the entire funeral process step by step so nothing is missing here:

☐ _____
☐ _____
☐ _____
☐ _____
☐ _____
☐ _____
☐ _____
☐ _____
☐ _____
☐ _____
☐ _____
☐ _____
☐ _____
☐ _____
☐ _____
☐ _____
☐ _____
☐ _____
☐ _____
☐ _____
☐ _____
☐ _____
☐ _____
☐ _____
☐ _____
☐ _____
☐ _____
☐ _____
☐ _____

ALL MY LIFE

- [ ] _____
- [ ] _____
- [ ] _____
- [ ] _____
- [ ] _____
- [ ] _____
- [ ] _____
- [ ] _____
- [ ] _____
- [ ] _____
- [ ] _____
- [ ] _____
- [ ] _____
- [ ] _____
- [ ] _____
- [ ] _____
- [ ] _____
- [ ] _____
- [ ] _____
- [ ] _____
- [ ] _____
- [ ] _____
- [ ] _____
- [ ] _____
- [ ] _____
- [ ] _____
- [ ] _____
- [ ] _____
- [ ] _____

FUNERAL ARRANGEMENTS

☐ #4: I have a few instructions of my own to be included in my funeral arrangements.

ALL MY LIFE

A QUOTE TO LIVE BY

You have brains, feet, and you can steer yourself in any direction you choose.

You are the one who'll decide where to go.

DR. SEUSS

CHAPTER 15
MY LIFE'S STORY & OBITUARY

I think my life's journal will be incomplete without me narrating the story of my life. How it all started, some major events, and the things I did throughout my life. Don't worry, I won't bore you, in fact, I will keep it short & sweet, and mention only the most important events. So, here it goes:

_____

_____

_____

_____

_____

_____

_____

MY LIFE'S STORY & OBITUARY

ALL MY LIFE

MY LIFE'S STORY & OBITUARY

ALL MY LIFE

MY LIFE'S STORY & OBITUARY

☐ #2: Please publish my obituary so everybody knows that I am no longer among them. Use a pretty picture ok, I want to look good! Here are the details about my obituary:

A QUOTE TO LIVE BY

Never let your sense of morals prevent you from

doing what is right.

ISAAC ASIMOV

CHAPTER 16
THE DONOR

One day, I came across an organization that was striving towards healing people and helping them live a healthy life. One of the areas where they were lagging was the organ department. There are millions of people who need help and I wanted to contribute to this great cause. I know one person's organs won't end the problem, but it could be a start from my own side. Besides, I don't think I will need these organs in the afterlife, I can get new ones there, can't I? In any case, I request you to contact the organization and give them the news; invite them saying "the deliverables are ready." Here are the contact details and information about the organization.

☐ #1: Details of the organ donation trust. Please contact them and fulfill their procedures.

- Organization's Name:

_____

- Address:

_____

_____

- Manager's Name:

_____

- Contact:

_____

☐ #2: Additional information about the donation agreement:

_____

_____

_____

_____

_____

ALL MY LIFE

A QUOTE TO LIVE BY

You must learn from the mistakes of others.

You can't possibly live long enough to make them all yourself.

SAM LEVENSON

CHAPTER 17
MY FINAL THOUGHTS

As I am reaching the end, there are a cluster of thoughts rising within my mind. I want to respect them and empty the vessel by pouring every word into the following pages:

_____

_____

_____

_____

_____

_____

_____

_____

_____

MY FINAL THOUGHTS

ALL MY LIFE

MY FINAL THOUGHTS

:
ALL MY LIFE

MY FINAL THOUGHTS

ALL MY LIFE

✪✪✪✪✪

*If you like this book, please **leave a review on Amazon** because it will help me improve it in the future and help other people just like you to narrate their final words.*

A QUOTE TO LIVE BY

Honest criticism is hard to take, particularly from a relative, a friend, an acquaintance, or a stranger.

FRANKLIN P. JONES

CHAPTER 18
FAREWELL WISHES

I wouldn't have done it without my beloved family members and my supportive friends. I owe you guys; when you get here, we will celebrate in my heavenly castle. But please, no rush, take your time.

I would like to say...

_____

_____

_____

_____

_____

_____

_____

_____

ALL MY LIFE

FAREWELL WISHES

ALL MY LIFE

FAREWELL WISHES

ALL MY LIFE

FAREWELL WISHES

_____

_____

_____

_____

_____

_____

_____

_____

_____

_____

_____

_____

_____

_____

_____

_____

_____

Keep Smiling and live your life to the fullest.

I will be watching!

A QUOTE TO LIVE BY

It's okay to look at the past and the future.

Just don't stare.

FRANKLIN P. JONES

EXTRA NOTES

I think I have said everything, but if I forget something and have to add it to the journal, then I will be including it in this section.

☐ #1: Please check this box after reading and understanding the extra thoughts.

_____
_____
_____
_____
_____
_____
_____
_____

EXTRA NOTES

EXTRA NOTES

EXTRA NOTES

EXTRA NOTES

❋ THANK YOU, IT WAS ONE HAPPY LIFE ❋